ACTIONABLE AGILE TOOLS

Tools that make a difference
Practical tips from more than 10 years of AGILE

WHAT OTHERS ARE SAYING ABOUT ACTIONABLE AGILE TOOLS, THE BOOK

"Started implementing the #actionableagiletools in our organization and for our clients."

– *Geroges Hanna @Articoz*

"I like the idea of "Experiment Drive Change". Also, the idea of "Tasty Timeboxes" of #actionableagiletools is great for encouraging informal communication."

– *Matthias Günther @wikimatze*

"Just finished reading and highly recommend #actionableagiletools by Jeff Campbell (@Zebra_003)."

– *Tyler Dean Smith @thatguy666*

ACTIONABLE AGILE TOOLS

Tools that make a difference
Practical tips from more than 10 years of AGILE

JEFF CAMPBELL

ACTIONABLE AGILE TOOLS
Copyright © 2017 by Jeff Campbell.

All rights reserved. This book or any portion thereof may not be reproduced or used in any manner whatsoever without the express written permission of the publisher except for the use of brief quotations in a book review.

Publisher: Oikosofy Series,
www.oikosofyseries.com

Cover art by Ivan Kurylenko.
https://www.instagram.com/hortasar.covers

Contents

Foreword 7
Purpose Of This Book 9
Some Practical Stuff 11
Experiment Driven Change 13
Door Calendar 19
Doing Dots 23
Bugs for Breakfast 27
Communication Protocol 29
Tasty Timeboxes 33
Where Does The Time Go? 35
Event Log 39
Resilience Map 41
Recruitment Retrospectives 45
Appreciation Flowers 51
Value Poker 53
In-Line Definition of Done 57
Not Now Backlog 59
Visualised Flow 63
Morning Meeting Protocol 71
Work In Progress Protocol 75

Foreword

When Jeff handed me this book I loved the concept and wanted to read it right away. I'm always looking for practical techniques to help others become more effective in their work.

I was getting ready for a long trip home so I put it into my backpack to read while traveling. I'm glad I did. As I settled in for an overnight flight I opened it up and started reading - and I read it cover to cover.

At first, it seemed like a straightforward book sharing some simple yet innovative techniques and practices, but by the time I was done with it I had recognized it as something more meaningful than that. It's about learning how we can create and collect our own set of practices.

In this book Jeff has provided a wonderful embodiment of this quote from Peter Block: "The value of another's experience is to give us hope, not to tell us how or whether to proceed."

Each tool and tip that Jeff shares is based on real "in the trenches" experience, and can be used right out of the box. But more than that they give us hope and a starting point as we explore and create just the right technique for any situation we find ourselves in.

My suggestion: Read the whole book, internalize the ideas, experiment with each one that fits a need you have, tune and adjust based on what you learn, and use them to spark new ideas as you innovate your own set of tips and tools.

Woody Zuill
Software Industry veteran
www.MobProgramming.org
http://zuill.us/WoodyZuill

Purpose Of This Book

I have been helping teams and organisations to adopt Agile ways of working for close to 10 years now, usually as a Scrum Master or Agile Coach. During this time, I have had the privilege of working with many great teams, and being exposed to a lot of different environments. This exposure has been a brilliant learning experience, as each organisation is unique and it therefore forced me to try new things and approaches in my efforts to support change. In this book, I share the Agile toolkit I developed over the last decade.

Many of these tools were developed incrementally within teams I worked with, some of these tools took several years and exposure to a variety of organisations to reach their current state.

Agile is a about how to think more than it is about particular tools or practices, but sometimes you just need a starting point to solve a problem you have and a simple tool to get you started will make a big difference. The purpose of this book is to help you get started solving those problems with tested tools that have worked with many teams before.

Most of these tools are very simple and can be implemented in less time than it takes to read about them but beware, the last thing you want to do is take all the tools in this book and start implementing them tomorrow. Some tools will only help in a specific context and every one of these tools requires that all individuals affected are on board with any change.

The first chapter in this book is about what I call "Experiment Driven Change"; you should consider this as the basis for the book and apply its principles when trying any of the other tools. The experimental approach has been instrumental to my career and has driven the creation of all the tools that come after it in the book.

Some Practical Stuff

Credit

At the end of each chapter, I will credit the people that created and helped me develop the tools in this book.

Assumptions

This book assumes that the reader has basic knowledge of Agile practices, as well as experience working in Agile teams. If this is your first book about Agile, I would recommend that you complement this book with the following books:

Scrum and XP from the trenches by Henrik Kniberg, which you can download here: https://www.infoq.com/minibooks/scrum-xp-from-the-trenches-2

Kanban and Scrum Minibook by...
https://www.infoq.com/minibooks/kanban-scrum-minibook

Images

Due to size restrictions, we cannot include in this book the full-resolution images of the tools. For a full-resolution copy of all images in this book, go here:
http://links.rebelalliance.se/actionable-agile-tools

Open Source

The content in this book is also an open source project, available at: https://github.com/Zebra003/actionable-agile-tools

The content for the project above is licensed under the Creative Commons "AttributionShareAlike 3.0 Unported" license. http://creativecommons.org/licenses/by-sa/3.0/deed.en_US
In practice, this means that you can modify and reuse the

contents in GitHub in anyway (even commercially) as long are you give credit, and allow others to do that same with your work.

Experiment Driven Change

The ability to continuously improve the way we work is critical for all Agile teams and organisations. Most teams use Retrospectives or similar improvement focused meetings, but far too often, those meetings follow an unproductive pattern.

- Put a bunch of stickies up on the board
- Talk about what is written on the stickies
- Create a list of 10-15 problems.
- Agree that all those 10-15 problems need to be resolved
- Give the list to the Scrum Master or mail them to a manager
- Come back in a few weeks and have the same discussion again

The team repeats this cycle for a few months or years until finally someone in the team has the courage to say "Why do we even do this? Nothing changes!"

If you are following this pattern, you are missing out on the value of Retrospectives. The most valuable thing about Retrospectives is the frequency at which we have them. This allows us to do things differently than we would in something like a project post mortem.

If you feel frustrated, if you feel that the time spent in Retrospectives is wasted time that would be better used doing "real work", then consider moving to Experiment Driven Change.

Focus

Since we frequently hold Retrospectives, we don't have to treat a Retrospective as the only meeting where we can identify all that's wrong in our organisation. Instead, we can focus on identifying only one impediment or problem and try to solve that. The focus that comes from choosing one single problem in the Retrospective meeting has an important mental effect: focusing on all the problems we have is exhausting and overwhelming, but focusing on one problem only allows us to feel like the issues are more manageable, even possible to solve relatively quickly.

Experiment

But the biggest benefit of holding frequent Retrospectives is the approach we can take to solving the impediments that affect us. Frequent Retrospectives allow for experimentation: we don't need to find the perfect solution to the issue we are discussing, we don't need to form committees and build consensus across our organisation. As a matter of fact, we don't even need to know if our solution will work at all.

Because we are working with such small increments, we only need to come up with something to try out in the next few weeks: an experiment.

And because we are only going to give the experiment a limited amount of time, any negative side-effect is limited by the fact that when we meet again, we will be able to detect that negative side-effect and stop the experiment.

On the other hand, if the experiment happens to make things better: well, now we are on our way!

The focus of a Retrospective is not to fix all our problems overnight; the only thing we are aiming for is to make the next few weeks slightly better than the ones before. Gradually, as more of these experiments work we will start to feel their cumulative impact.

Output

Here is a very simple format I use to attempt to arrive at experiments that we can run, and understand well.

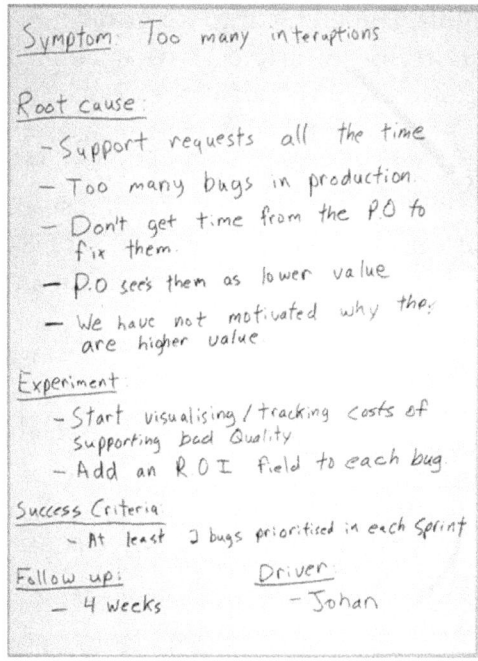

Figure 1 - Example experiment created with the team

Symptom

This is the "one thing" we have chosen to focus on, the symptom of the problem we want to solve. I always like to proceed from the premise that this symptom is merely one of an underlying issue, and it is the underlying issue that we need to solve, at least in the long run.

As a team, you can find and agree on what is this "one thing" in a variety of ways; most Retrospective formats provide a facilitation technique to arrive at the most important symptom. One possible technique is dot voting. Have the team vote on the symptom they want to tackle first.

> **In the example:** "Too many interruptions", which happens to be a common issue for software development teams!

Root Cause

Rather than simply launching into solution mode, we want to spend some time trying to arrive at what could be causing the symptom we prioritised. We call it the root cause. We can use many tools to help us find the root cause; in the example illustrated in Figure 1, we used a tool called "5 Whys", but there are many other possible alternatives. The most important aspect of finding a root cause is that we are open, honest, and dig a bit deeper, instead of accepting the symptom as the problem.

> **In the example:** We realised that most of these interruptions were caused by the need to support bad quality code in production. We then took the common approach of blaming others "THEY won't let us fix the quality!" Eventually, after more discussion, we decided that we did not explain very well why fixing the quality was so important.

Experiment

The Experiment step is where we decide on specific actions we should take to attempt to solve the root cause during the upcoming Sprint. While we would like to achieve consensus in defining these steps, we don't need consensus to run an experiment, we merely need everyone to be willing to accept that we will run this experiment and see if it works in practice.

> **In the example:** We will be trying to put some numbers on the cost of these errors so that we can better motivate their priority.

Success Criteria

How will we know this experiment worked?

We don't want to simply know that we have executed the

experiment. That will not ensure that there was any improvement just that we did what we said we would do. It's important and motivating for the team to have something measurable come out of the experiment. However, that doesn't mean we need any complex metrics, a measurement can be as simple as a majority of the team members agreeing that this was a successful experiment.

> **In the example:** Since we really want to fix some of the issues which caused the regular interruptions, we decided that the number of bugs prioritised was a good measurement for the impact of our experiment and an ultimate solution to the root cause we identified in Figure 1.

Follow up

How long will we wait for the results of the experiment before we evaluate its success? Set a date for when you will review the results of the experiment.

Driver

The driver is a person that reminds the team they must live up to their commitment to run the experiment. The driver is not responsible to do all the work; but rather to help the team take ownership of the experiment. The reason for having a driver is very simple: it's easy to forget the experiments we agreed upon when our heads are back in the code, or running around talking to stakeholders.

Repeat

And that's it!

Do I know this change will work? No.

Do you know what won't work? Doing nothing…

Tips

- Learn more about Retrospectives to make best use of this tool. (Check a free 10 day, step-by-step program to get you to host better Retrospectives here: bit.ly/freeretrospectivesprogram)
- Use different methods to arrive at "the one thing" to focus on.
- Vary the tools used to define the root causes.
- Timebox the Retrospective meeting and each of the steps to come up with the experiment.
- Spend more time on root cause than time creating the experiments because that's where most the value is, and where the insights come from.
- Use the Experiment Driven Change tool in one of the Retrospectives you facilitate to see if there are any improvements you can make to it or your use of it.
- Never "volunteer" someone else to act as driver.

- In many teams the Scrum Master ends up acting as the driver by default, this is an issue as teams need to feel responsible for their own improvement.

Credit: The specific in this are done by myself, but this concept has been around long enough. I wouldn't even hazard a guess at who invented it.

Door Calendar

Why Door Calendar I hear you ask. Well, the name came about because it turns out the door is often a convenient place to put a calendar, at least it was for me and on three completely different occasions.

Sometimes with our heads down focusing on delivering value it can be easy to lose sight of what's coming up next that we should take into account. Another example of the importance of a visible calendar was when we had certain events that happened at irregular intervals, such as holidays or company events. Another case when big visible calendars are necessary is if the Sprint Review sneaks up on you every time!

This is where the Door Calendar comes in.

The Door Calendar is a simple information radiator[1] that helps us see when events are approaching so that we are not surprised by them or forget to prepare for them. A picture really illustrates the concept best, so I'll start with that.

---

[1] For the origins of the word:
https://www.agilealliance.org/glossary/information-radiators/

Figure 2 - Door Calendar

The calendar is constructed using tape, a marker and sticky notes. The top row includes days of the week. Each cell on the calendar is large enough to hold a sticky note. These notes are added with some small text to indicate the event. A different colored note is used to indicate "today". You can have week numbers (in Sweden – the country where I spend most of my time - everyone loves week numbers) or dates along one side.

During your daily meeting the "today" note is moved and new events are added. At the start of each week everything is moved up one row so we can see a bit further.

Updating it as a team makes sure we talk about the most important events coming up and they don't sneak up on anyone as the whole team sees the events approaching, but it is also brilliant at starting discussions: "Oy Jeff! What's that Lan Party about?" – asked my manager ;). Or:

"Oh, is the customer putting that feature into production

tomorrow? Should we have some extra support available just in case?"

"The big company party is coming in the next Sprint, we should be sure to plan a little less capacity for our next Sprint"

Tips

- Get in the habit of having everyone check the calendar at the same time when the "today" marker is moved, it only takes a few seconds and adds a lot of value.
- Use different colour notes to indicate different types of activities like normal cadence meetings, holidays, one off, or extra important events.
- Don't be shy about putting fun things like outings and team events up there.
- Add the day of the month to the week # column to help out those who are not familiar with the week numbering system.
- Keep it simple! Don't make it any more complicated than described here, it easily gets cumbersome to update.
- The first version I created had laminated cards that could be reused and moved to indicate holidays, it was a pain and took WAY too much time for the initial setup.
- Keep the weekends visible, hopefully you never need them, but they also serve to break things up a bit and make it easier to quickly get a visual understanding.

Credit: I was part of the team that created this Agile tool. A brilliant team of consultants I worked with in Örebro, Sweden. You can find the company here: http://www.Nethouse.se

Doing Dots

Partially done work is a tremendous source of waste in the IT industry. This partially done work usually takes the form of items that never move on your task board. You know the ones, the stickies you don't even see anymore because they have been on the board long enough that your brain adds a filter that blocks them out.

These items are a much more serious issue than most people think because they represent an investment that has not been realised. We have put time and energy into these items, but we have not received the intended value from them as they have not been finished. Think about it, even if you put in very little time, just getting the note up on the wall required some planning, discussion, and labour. All these items represent a cost but have no value because they are not ready to be released. Items like these actually have negative value unless they are delivered to production.

These items are sometimes unimportant and should simply be thrown away, usually because they have been there so long the value has been lost. But more often than we would like to admit, these are items that have gotten blocked because of something which is not trivial to resolve. They are easily identified through conversations like:

> "What's up with task X?" "Well, I sent an email, and I'm still waiting to hear back."

> "Any movement on X?" "It's sitting in department Y, and you know how they are…"

Or the worst one in my opinion:
> "This one is basically done, I am just waiting for the OK from the customer before I move it".

I once had a team that had a "customer approval" column on their board, which was absolutely covered in notes. When we decided to follow up these notes, it turned out most of the time the customer didn't know they were being waited on. One of the customers had actually gone to another supplier because they got fed up with waiting!

By leaving items in a blocked status, we are not addressing the underlying issues that allowed them to become blocked in the first place and creating the possibility for future items to become blocked because of the same root cause.

Doing Dots won't actually fix this issue for you, but it will make it more visible and hopefully a bit harder to ignore.

It goes like this: an item gets a new dot for every day it spends in a stage. Easy as that! Takes a few seconds every day. Here's an example:

Figure 3 - Two different styles of Doing Dots

Eventually, these items get absolutely covered in dots, and we start asking questions of ourselves that we might never have asked otherwise:

"Is there anything we can do to get this moving again?"

"Is this item actually valuable?"

"How can we stop this from happening next time?"

At the very least, we will take notice of the item for the very brief time it requires to add the dot each day so we can't just move it lower and lower until it eventually falls off and gets thrown in the trash.

Tips

- Tally up the dots to provide the cycle time of the whole process.
- Use different colour dots for each stage; they can be tallied to provide a stage cycle time of your work.
- Visually highlight the blocker ticket by using other symbols like "?" and "!".
- Take the items with the most ticks to your retrospective and try to find common causes, and of course ways to address them.

Credit: I learned this one from a video by Paul Klipp. (http://www.paulklipp.com). https://www.youtube.com/watch?v=8X3SbHmWzGo

Bugs for Breakfast

People often say that quality is essential to the success of Agile teams. What they really mean is that quality is essential for any long standing team and we choose to focus on Agile teams. But how do you keep quality top of mind? How do you make sure quality issues aren't being ignored or down prioritised such as to be effectively ignored?

You eat Bugs for Breakfast!

We want to be moving towards a defect free environments and making sure that quality is simply built in, but many teams are not there yet. Bugs for breakfast is a technique that helps teams along that journey to the defect free utopia we dream of.

Bugs for breakfast is a meeting where the team spends some time together eating breakfast and socialising, but this time is also used to increase our quality focus. During this meeting, we take some time to examine whatever quality indicators of quality we have in the team; this could be error logs from the servers, bug reports from customers, defects found by testers, our issue tracker, or any other quality indicator that you might already have. We then try to find trends and groupings of issues so we can plan to take a bite out of whatever the biggest ones are.

You can then plan to take these things back to your Sprint, make them highest priority on your Kanban board, or simply sit as a team and address some of them right there in the room. The important part here is that you not only look at the quality metrics and defects, but use this meeting as a platform to motivate the team to do something about improving quality.

Eventually when your breakfasts have had a big enough impact, the jump to zero defects is a much simpler one. And when people ask you how is it possible that you have no bugs you can say: "Bugs!?! My team eats bugs for breakfast!" Don't all teams want to say that? ☺

Tips

- Start with an timebox of one hour, once a week.
- Have defects printed or on sticky notes that you bring to the breakfast meeting to make the grouping of bugs a more engaging activity.
- If your company won't pay for the breakfast, just ask each team member to contribute a small amount to make it happen.
- If you're a Scrum Master, make this extra easy for your team by sorting the breakfast aspect for them.
- Look for things to resolve that have a good ROI, so that the stakeholders see the benefits of this practice and allow the team more time to address the next defects on the list. Remember that zero defects is what we are shooting for!

Credit: I was part of the team that created this Agile tool. A brilliant team of consultants I worked with in Örebro, Sweden. You can find the company here: http://www.Nethouse.se

Communication Protocol

Striking the right balance in communication can be very tricky. In Agile teams we value face-to-face communication because it's high bandwidth and enables rapid feedback. But face-to-face communication can cause a lot of interruptions, and may even cause tension to break out in the team.

If you feel you are having trouble striking the right balance, try getting a Communication Protocol in place.

A Retrospective is a great place to introduce and develop this practice with the team.

Start with an introduction, explain to the team that you will talk about how and why you communicate with each other, and to decide on your rules of communication, so that team members are interrupted less and have higher quality conversations.

Remind everyone that all decisions are experiments, so no one needs to feel like they will be locked in by a decision they don't agree with. We will simply bring it up again and try something else if someone can't live with a long term decision.

I like to have a quick round table about how people feel communication is working within the team at that time. This helps everyone open up, and gives us an idea if there is a problem and where it might be.

Next, have an open brainstorming session about what are situations in which people need to communicate face-to-face with one another. I just ask people to shout out suggestions, I write them down on individual sticky notes and put them up on the whiteboard. This further encourages open discussion, and allows team members to build off each other's ideas.

After this open discussion we have a list of reasons to communicate, and then we need to define and agree how we communicate. Have the team discuss and list the different communication practices we have. Some common examples are:

- Face-to-face
- Daily standup
- Team chat room
- Email
- Issue tracker
- The board
- Planning
- The Retrospective meeting
- The Review meeting

Then have a brief discussion about the benefits and drawbacks of each of these, write them down separately for future reference.

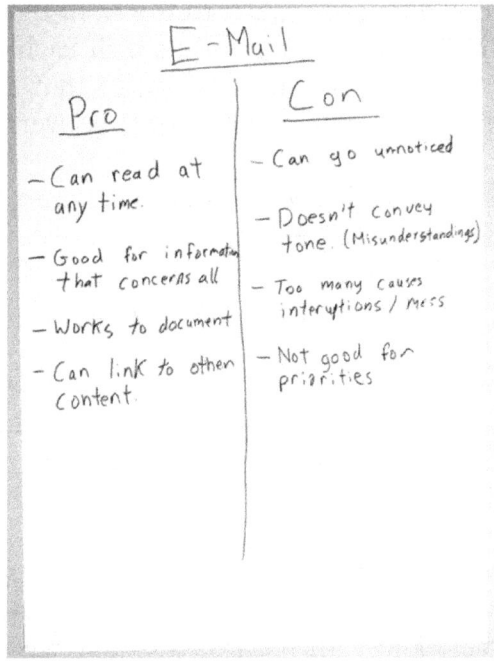

Figure 4 - Pros and Cons for e-mail communication

Use each communication practice that come up here as a heading on the whiteboard and ask everyone to start grouping the different circumstances that require communication under them (see Figure 5 for an example). When there is disagreement as to when a specific communication practice should be used, we have a discussion around that specific practice. If it can be resolved quickly, great. If not, move them to a "parking lot" until the end of the meeting.

Once you have grouped all the practices people can agree on, move on to the ones that were not trivial to resolve. Allow a short timebox to discuss each one, but if in the end an agreement can't be reached, use a simple voting system (fist of five or dot voting) to decide the initial state and mark that item as disputed. This will help people who didn't get their way to feel a little bit better and make sure you follow up in a few weeks how well the agreement for that practice is working.

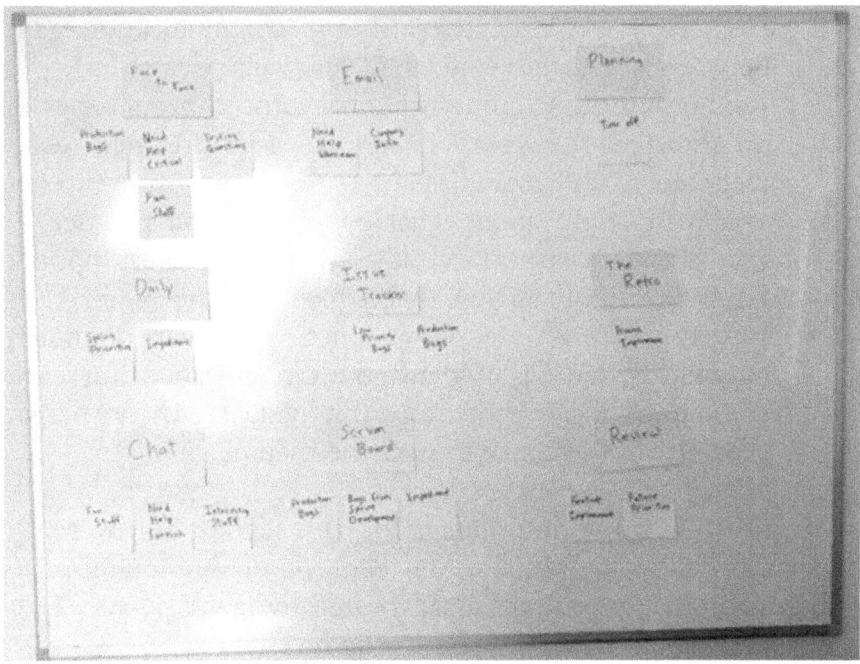

Figure 5 - Communication Protocol: communication circumstances listed under each communication practice

You now have a Communication Protocol! You'll probably want to make it visible in the team room. The true value of this is in the discussions it spawns, not the actual output. Things like:

"I really hate when I get interrupted by testing questions?"
"But don't you think it's important to test the things we build?"

"Sometimes I feel awkward interrupting people, because I am so new and need to do it so often"

"Onboarding new people is very important for us, we don't mind if you interrupt us at all! Also, we should probably be pairing with you more"

Tips

- If you don't have a team chat room (e.g. Skype, Slack, IRC, etc.), get one, they fill the communication gaps between face-to-face and email very well.
- Rephrasing the Communication Protocol into a series of questions and answers makes it easier for new team members to understand.
- When in doubt about what communication practice to use, choose face-to-face, it's always the safest option. Later on you can change that agreement if necessary.
- In groups that are very quiet, or have dominant individuals, have people list the circumstances for each communication practice as an individual activity so that everyone has a chance to state their views.

Credit: The specific details of this agile tool were developed by myself, but the concept of developing a communication protocol is advocated by many people, I wouldn't even hazard a guess at who invented it.

Tasty Timeboxes

You often find yourself wanting to refer to past sprints or iterations. Maybe you want to communicate to stakeholders when in the past something was released or built, maybe you want to remind the team of a specific situation ("remember how awesome Sprint 42 was?"), or for many other reasons.

Different people solve this in various ways; the simplest being to number sprints, others name the sprints after the goals and others pick a theme, like gemstones or chemical elements. But I like to take it one step further with a tool I call Tasty Timeboxes!

Tasty Timeboxes work just like a normal naming convention; you start with "A" and iterate through the alphabet. But Tasty Timeboxes take this one step further by using something the whole team likes to eat - baked goods, for example, apple pie, blueberry crumble, cherry cheesecake, and devil's food cake.

At your review meeting, at the end of each Sprint, you not only get to look at the amazing working software you built and collect valuable feedback, but you get to eat something tasty together with all your stakeholders and teammates! What could be a better morale booster?

When working with the first team who used this tool, we had our customers visit every two weeks for the Sprint Review. You would host the Review and then take a break to eat cake together. So, it also had the added benefit of helping our customer relations and encouraging informal communication. For a while, we even had a tradition team members baking the things we ate.

Obviously, cakes are not the only option. Cheeses, fruits, ice creams, and candy all work well. The options really are endless.

It's also kind of fun when you get to tricky letters like X, Y, Z.

I theorise you are building a conditioned response to being happy about review meetings, but this is based purely on my own pseudo-science, I have no actual data to back it up.

Tips

- Pick something that the entire team thinks is nice to share during the Review meeting.
- If you want to vote on what it should be, get a simple system in place. Otherwise, you may end up in silly arguments costing more than they are worth.
- After a while, it can be hard to get volunteers to bake or prepare the item, and some people feel they are always volunteering while others do not. I prefer to just buy the things. And I even know an amazing bakery down the road that bakes the most amazing Cranberry Cheesecake! ☺ I'm always excited to attend the Review of the third sprint of every team I work with.

Credit: I was part of the team that created this agile tool. A brilliant team of consultants I worked with in Örebro, Sweden. You can find the company here: http://www.Nethouse.se

WHERE DOES THE TIME GO?

Does it feel like you never have any time to focus on your most important work? Do you feel like time just disappears and you don't know how or why? Are you sure there are too many meetings but can't convince others? Do you spend more time than you feel you should on wasteful activities?

Then you should start figuring out Where Does The Time Go?

It's very important in creative activities, such as software development, that we get large chunks of uninterrupted time. This enables us to get into a flow and really be productive and innovative. But far too often we find we only get an hour or two here and there.

When trying to motivate why something has to change it's always good to bring data. This simple tracking system can help you do that.

First, decide on a few different categories for time. Here are some that I like to use, but you should decide on these with your team.

- Planned
    - The work you had planned to accomplish.
- Support
    - Cost of poor quality or usability.
- Critical
    - Unplanned work that was deemed to be critical.
- Meetings
    - Time spent in meetings.
- Administration
    - Things like creating reports, time reporting, etc.

Don't bother clearly defining exactly what each is used for from the start. You can solve these questions as they come up.

At the daily meeting take a moment for each team member to tick the categories they worked on during the previous day. The numbers don't need to be precise, just close enough.

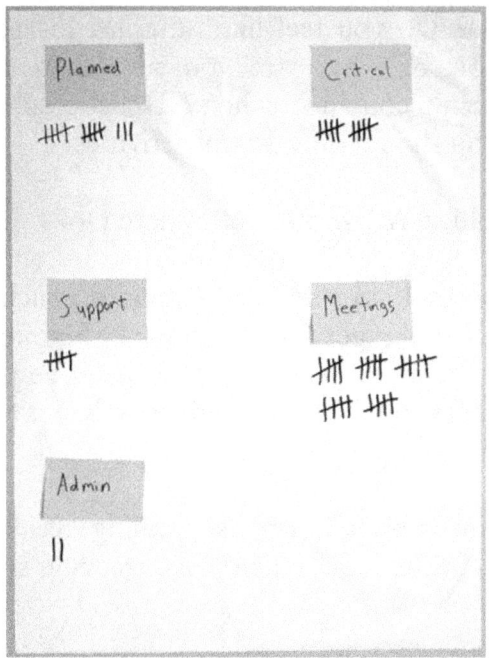

Figure 6 - Where the time goes: example of how to track time according to work category

Compile the numbers every so often and wipe the chart clean.

You will now have data to motivate the things that you feel are wasteful, and you might even discover time is being spent in ways you never even suspected.

I once worked in a team that used this tool to look at costs related to deployment. The team was able to use this data to motivate the company to heavily invest in automated deployment and testing processes. With another team, we used this data to reduce the amount of work in progress at the same time. We were able to do this because we showed our stakeholders the large communication overhead which was eating up all the available time.

Tips

- Take this along to Retrospectives to discuss value adding and non-value adding activities.
- Make it very clear to the team that this is not a time tracking tool.
- Use sticky notes for the categories so they can be added or removed.
- If there is something specific you want to remember you can add a sticky note under the category to remind you of it when the retrospective rolls around.
- Track the data over periods of time to see trends.

Credit: As far as I am aware, this one was developed by me. If you know of a similar tool, ping me so that I can add here the right credit to other authors.

Event Log

Do you ever get into the Retrospective and the team realises they only really remember the last few days of the current sprint? Do you find that important events do not always get brought up at the retrospective?

A simple tool I call the Event Log can help with this.

All you need is to mount a large piece of paper (A1) near your Sprint or Kanban board. I personally like these: http://www.magicwhiteboard.co.uk/

Each day at your daily meeting you take a moment to write down things from the previous day that people feel are important to remember at the Review or Retrospective meetings.

```
Sprint Carrot Cake
13/03 - Deployed to P
14/03 - 40 support requests
15/03 - Deployed bug fix to P
        - with automated tests
20/03 - 0 support requests
22/03 - Server's rebooting ?!?
```

Figure 7 - Example Event Log for a team

This Event Log can then be brought along to the Retrospective either as it is, or compiled into a timeline. A quick glance is enough to recall events that would otherwise be forgotten and never discussed.

Also, the act of reflecting every day in and of itself provides benefit because we take time to focus on the previous day before we move onto the next one!

Tips

- Update the Event Log as part of a daily ritual. Every time I tried to just "update it whenever you think of something" it has not been successful.
- You can also use it to quickly gather other data such as:
  - Team happiness
  - Confidence in the plan
  - Amount of quality issues
  - Don't do too much of this at once, you don't want it to become a chore.
- Encourage putting successes up there as well. It's very easy for this to simply be a list of "issues" from the week.
- You can use it to define a focus for the retrospectives as well, by simply dot voting on the events.

Credit: I was part of the team that created this agile tool. A brilliant team of consultants I worked with in Örebro, Sweden. You can find the company here: http://www.Nethouse.se

Resilience Map

We often talk about Cross-functional teams, and T-Shaped people. There are a lot of benefits to these approaches. For example, the work is much less likely to be blocked due to a bottleneck in a specific skill or competence. Teams that can take work completely from idea to production, have less handovers, and are resilient to unexpected events. Additionally, team members will always come and go, and single ownership of a competence is a huge risk for any team, aka the Bus Factor.

But how do we go about reducing this risk? What do we focus on first?

Have you noticed how in the planning meeting you need to take something of lower priority because there is not enough capacity in one type of competence? Do you often find yourself saying "That's a typical Sebastian task"? Do you worry that if one person leaves you will not be able to manage a specific system because only that one person can work with that system?

If this is the case then you could try out a Resilience Map.

This is one of those cases where a picture says more than a thousand words:

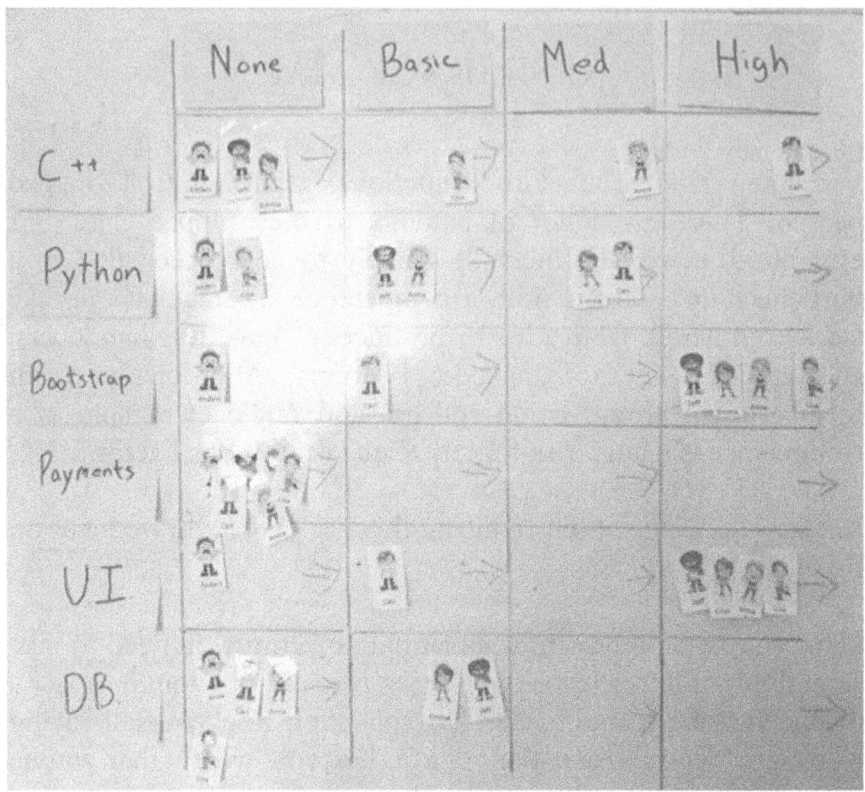
Figure 8 - Example Resilience Map

It's a fairly simple information radiator created by the team. Along the Y axis we have the technical competences or areas of our product, and along the X axis we have the level of comfort in that area. Then we have avatars representing each team member.

At a glance I can see:
- We have a very serious issue in the payment area of our product, we had better start focusing on doing something about that.
- In the UI and related technologies, we have a lot of resilience so, maybe we don't need to train any of our team members in this competence area.
- Anders, whose avatar is the only one in the "none" column for all skills, needs support because he doesn't feel confident in any of these areas.
- I can also easily see the best person to talk with, if ever I

don't feel comfortable in a certain area.

The Resilience Map won't actually make us more resilient, but it will clearly show us where there is a problem. This is the first step in addressing any problem.

Tips

- Take this along to the Retrospectives to shine a light on competence and skill sharing topics.
- Take this along to planning sessions to make it easier to consider your gaps and their possible effect.
- Use this to motivate to your Product Owner or stakeholders why a backlog item is worked on even if it has lower priority than another item that you are not working on.
- Use this daily when defining who to pair with.
- Don't put every skill/competence in the Resilience Map, it will become too much to read and maintain, focus only on the highest priority skills or competences.
- Choose a regular interval at which to update this, not just the avatars but the focus areas along the Y axis.
- Consider if your organisation is ready for this level of openness, if anyone in the team is nervous about the reaction, keep it as a private tool until the team feels comfortable sharing this with the other teams and the rest of the organisation.

Credit: As far as I am aware, this one was developed by me. If you know of a similar tool ping me so that I add here the right credit to other authors.

Recruitment Retrospectives

Before I get into what it is, a few horror stories to provide context.

1) In one of my first ever office jobs, I showed up to work on my first day bright eyed and optimistic. But there was no place for me to sit. I was told my desk and chair were in a box somewhere around the office, I should track them down and put them together. Next, I was tasked with scrounging parts to make sure I had a computer to work on.

What did I learn from this?

This company is totally making it up as they go, and it's fine for me to do the same.

What did the company learn from this? Nothing.

2) Another time I was brought into a truly monolithic company for a six month project. The work itself is not important to this story, however I was doing it as a consultant, so my time was not cheap. The same problem repeated itself: I did not have a computer to work on and their IT policies prevented me from using my own. Every day I would sit around for a few hours until the person I reported to would tell me to go home for the day. After a few days of this, he told me to stop coming in and he would call when the computer was ready. I explained that since I was not able to take other customers during this period I would have to charge them for the time, this was apparently fine. It took three weeks for the machine to arrive.

What did I learn from this?

This company is a huge lumbering beast that simply throws money away, you could hide here the rest of your life and get paid if you wanted to.

What did the company learn from this? Nothing.

3) Later I was asked to take the role of Scrum Master for two teams in a semi large organisation. I was excited about this role, as I just came off the height of helping a truly brilliant team to improve their agility. I arrived on my first day and all the things with computers and desks and such went very smoothly. Then, I was introduced to the teams. They did not know I was coming, they were informed of my arrival while I was standing there. As were the people who I would be replacing...

What did I learn from this?

This company has no respect for people, and I should expect a lot of resistance to change.

What did the company learn from this? Nothing.

Stories like these are why we have the Recruitment Retrospective!

So that we don't miss the chance to learn from these stories, and so that we can use these mistakes as learning opportunities to improve ourselves and our organisations.

How we onboard people to our teams is incredibly important, not just because we want to get them up to speed quickly, but also because we want them to start off with the right momentum and carry on with it for as long as we work together. We want them to get the feeling "this company has its s#!7! together, that means I'd better as well".

I have a team who always does Mob Programming[2] when a new

---

[2] Mob programming is a software development approach where the whole

team member starts. The entire team gathers around one large screen and makes the new person's introduction the most important thing they have to do for as long as it takes. They make this person feel welcomed but more importantly, they make sure they get ALL the support could possibly need to have a great start.

But it's not the bad starts that are the problem, it's the lost learning opportunity that really fills me with disappointment. People never pay as much attention as they do in their first days, we need to make sure we have a way to learn about onboarding as it happens.

Setting up a Recruitment Retrospective is very simple. When a new person starts, the first step is to schedule a recurring follow up to capture their feedback on the hiring and onboarding process.

Some companies already do this, but the Recruitment Retrospective differs slightly from what most companies do.

First, it is driven by the person who has just been recruited (the new recruit). The rest of the organisation's job is to support them in this. The new recruit invites the people they believe are the most important to the retrospective depending on what they think is most important to improve, and the rest of the team gives them all the support they need. These could be organisational improvements with the onboarding process itself, or more team related things like how we share knowledge for example.

---

team works on the same thing, at the same time, in the same space, and at the same computer. https://en.wikipedia.org/wiki/Mob_programming

Secondly, experiments[3] are proposed to address these issues next time we hire someone. We do not simply make statements about "doing it better next time", but we state specifically what we will do and how. The concerned people agree to make sure these things happen next time and assess if they were successful or not.

You can attempt to improve the onboarding process as a new recruit, but the optimal solution is to have learning built into the company's culture and to embrace change.

Thirdly, this review and experiment process continues for at least the first few months so that the new recruit has the ability to continuously improve and therefore positively affect their introduction to the team. Keeping the process alive for a few months also helps find more learning opportunities, even ones not related to the onboarding process, but relevant for any new person that is not yet "tainted" by the problems that the team has decided to accept.

Finally, the new recruit is asked to assist the next person to be hired with their Recruitment Retrospectives.

What do you learn from this?

That this company is serious about improvement, that they value your input, that you can have a lasting impact on the way the company works, and that this is the place for you!

What does the company learn from this?

Everything necessary to make the onboarding a good experience for both the new recruit and their team.

Tips

---

[3] Check out the Experiment Driven Change chapter for ideas on how to setup these experiments.

- Provide the new recruit with a contact to turn to when they need help with an experiment or an improvement.
- Provide the new recruit with a contact who is experienced in Retrospectives and improvement initiatives, for example a Scrum Master or Agile Coach.
- Write things down. Since you are trying to improve the process for all future employees as well, it's good to document and follow up experiments.
- Periodically examine the onboarding process as a whole. With all the changes happening, it's possible that the onboarding process grows too large and complex.

Credit: As far as I am aware, this one was developed by me. But I was greatly inspired by a friend's blog post "Make the new guy the hero": https://kalleandmatte.wordpress.com/2012/05/15/day-1-checklist-make-the-new-guy-the-hero/

Appreciation Flowers

It feels nice to be appreciated.

It feels nice to know that your co-workers notice the little things you do.

It feels nice to get a pat on the back when you have done a particularly good job.

That's what Appreciation Flowers are all about; making people feel nice!

At your retrospective, have a section on the wall where people can post flowers to one another. A flower can be as simple as a Post-it with a person's name on it, although I like to make them a nice drawing of a flower as well.

These flowers are used to say a special thank you to someone.

Dedicate a few minutes to take up each note individually and ask the person who wrote it to say a few words about why they wrote it.

The recipient is given the flower to take back to their desk, or wherever they like.

While I used this tool, I've noticed that after a while, a bit of an arms race develops around the quality and size of the flowers. People started drawing more and more elaborate flowers on them to make their gifts extra special, to show special appreciation.

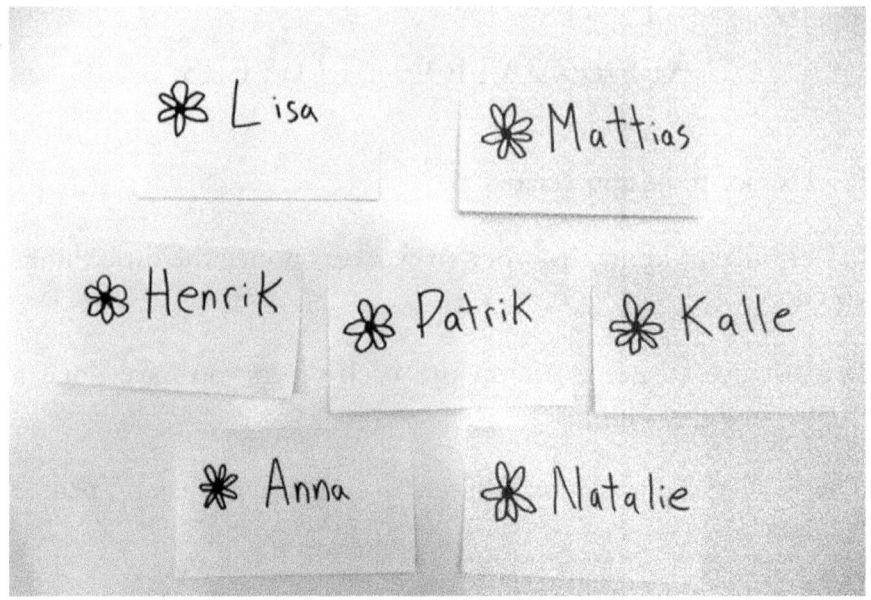

Figure 9 - A few crudely drawn flowers to some reviewers for this book.

Tips

- Give flowers to people outside the team as well; they always appreciate receiving them.
- Use the number of flowers given as an indicator of the mood in the team. More flowers mean the team is at ease and happy to engage in playful behaviour. Fewer flowers may mean that there are unaddressed issues in the team.

Credit: Many people are advocating this, one similar approach that springs to mind is Jurgen Appelo and his "Kudo Box". But the implementation just described was created by a brilliant team of consultants I worked with in Örebro, Sweden. You can find the company here: http://www.Nethouse.se

VALUE POKER

This tool assumes you are familiar with the technique of "Planning Poker". If not, take a glance at it first. (https://en.wikipedia.org/wiki/Planning_poker)

We talk a lot about value in Agile teams. Delivering value, prioritising by value, measuring value, but value is a very abstract concept. People perceive value differently. They value different things and have their own ways of reasoning about it. But if we are to prioritise our backlog based on ROI (cost vs. value) then we need a common view of the value of items. This is where Value Poker comes in!

Value Poker is a relative estimation technique because we don't actually need to know the exact value of items to prioritise them - just their value relative to the other items in our backlog.

Start by finding some baseline items, because to have a relative estimate, it needs to be relative to something. Start by selecting a few recently completed backlog items that have already started to deliver some value.

Find the right people

In Planning Poker, the team estimates the relative size and complexity of a story. In Value Poker, we are looking for the value of stories, which requires knowing who is able to help us quantify value. Make sure you involve the right stakeholders. There is no simple answer to who these people are, and it will vary from organisation to organisation, but my simple rule of thumb is to find the 6-10 people who understand the product the best and can make decisions regarding prioritisation.

But remember: the team building the product is as important a stakeholder as any other, and they will benefit from hearing the conversations about the value of each User Story or Feature.

Agree on the time scale

Some things only create value over a longer period of time; some things diminish in value as time goes on. We need to agree on what type of time scale we are referring to when we are talking about the value of an item. Is it a week? Is it a year? This will, of course, depend on your business context.

Find some 2's

- Find an item that is close to the lowest value in your backlog, not the lowest, but maybe the second lowest.
- Everyone must agree that they have a very good idea of the value of this item.
- Try to find something with a very clear value description. For example: this saves us X hours per week, or this pays us X amount of money a week.
- Arbitrarily assign this item a value of 2.

As we will be including different areas of our organisation, take the time to find several 2's that represent these various standpoints and perspectives in your organisation.
These items will be your Value Poker baseline!

Find some 5's

In order to confirm we have reached a baseline everyone agrees on, we want to find some more items we all agree on about double the value as the ones we just picked. The same rules as before apply:

- Everyone must agree that they have a very good idea of the value of this item.
- Try to find something with a very clear value description. For example: this saves us X hours per week, or this pays us X amount of money a week.

We have now confirmed our baseline!

Start Estimating Value

From this point on, Value Poker works just like Planning Poker.

- People each decide privately what they think the value of an item is. Using a non-linear scale, for example: 1, 2, 3, 5, 8, 13, 21, "Don't know".
- Everyone reveals their estimate at once.
- If everyone agrees we have the estimate;
- If there is disagreement, we must motivate to each other the reasoning behind our estimates and listen to others do the same.
- We repeat this process until the estimates converge or we decide to table the discussion. Hint: don't re-run the estimation for a single item more than twice. After that, just pick the number that best describes the group's view.

We now have a common unit with which we can prioritise. Ordering the backlog should now be trivial, right? Of course not, but it sure helps a lot now that we are all speaking about the same thing. Estimating value in this way, of course, lacks precision, but let's be honest, was the alternative of having no value estimates very precise?

The true value in this activity is around the discussions that spawn as a result of it.

Value Poker helps to build consensus among those involved in the discussion. It helps us reveal our assumptions, opens the floor to discussions about the value of the items in the backlog, and provides us with a metric to follow up the value achieved later on. Just like Planning Poker!

Tips

- Take some time to discuss the different ways in which we perceive value; time saved, money in, quality, customer loyalty, etc.

- Do a quick "bubble sort"[4] at the beginning of the discussion to make finding those 2's and 5's easier.
- Tell everyone the infinity card (if you use one) is only to be used in cases of "paradigm shifting" levels of value.
- Empower your Product Owner to make decisions in cases where the people involved agree that they will never be able to reach a consensus.
- Have everyone agree up front to abide by the Product Owner's decision in these cases.
- Periodically re-establish your baselines as your knowledge of value in your organisation evolves.

Credit: As far as I am aware, this one was developed by me. But the technique of Planning Poker is not. The method was first defined and named by James Grenning in 2002 and later popularised by Mike Cohn in the book Agile Estimating and Planning, whose company trademarked the term.

---

[4] Bubble sort is a sorting algorithm that uses pair-comparison as the mechanism to sort a list of items: https://en.wikipedia.org/wiki/Bubble_sort

In-Line Definition of Done

This tool assumes you are familiar with the Scrum tool "Definition of Done". If not, take a glance at it first. (http://www.scrumguides.org/scrum-guide.html#artifact-transparency-done)

Are you following your Definition of Done? Do you know what it contains? Are you often forgetting the small things you need to do when building your product? Is your current process prone to human error?

If so, you might consider using an In-Line Definition of Done to make that check-list more prominent in everybody's mind.

The Definition of Done keeps us honest in our teams because it prevents us from cutting corners whenever we like. But additionally, it also serves as a reminder of how our process works so that the small stuff is not forgotten.

Most teams have this posted prominently over the "Done" column of their board, but you would be surprised how this is easily ignored, especially in crunch time. If this is what is happening to you, try this:

- Break your Definition of Done into a short checklist.
- Create a template for the tasks and stories that you use on your board, include in this template the checklist items.
- Have a ceremony for checking off every item before tasks and stories move to the "Done" column.

Story Name	DoD
Details of Story	☐ Checked in and released ☐ All unit tests passing ☐ All acceptance tests passed ☐ NFR tests passing ☐ Automated regression tests in place for critical flows ☐ Help file created ☐ Demo done with Team ☐ Demo Done with PO ☐ Deployed to staging

Task Name	DoD
Details of Task	☐ Code Reviewed ☐ All unit tests passing ☐ Checked in ☐ New unit tests in place ☐ Refactored ☐ How to test notes created ☐ Informed all effected by API change

Figure 10 - Cards with Definition of Done

As simple as that!

Your Definition of Done is now harder to ignore.

Tips

- Sometimes the checklist won't make sense for every single item, get in the habit of crossing out the ones that don't fit. This will make sure it's an active decision to ignore them.
- If this happens too often with a particular Definition of Done item, consider removing it.
- Take the Definition of Done to your Retrospective and ask the question: "what can we automate from this list?".

Credit: I was part of the team that created this one. A brilliant team of consultants I worked with in Örebro, Sweden. You can find the company here: http://www.Nethouse.se

Not Now Backlog

Maintaining a Product Backlog can be a costly activity, and it gets more and more costly the larger the backlog becomes. Actually, the cost is not the worst part of having a large backlog, the real risk is that it will become so unruly that it won't be used to its potential.

A useful backlog looks a bit like this:

Figure 11 - Backlog refinement

At each "level" of the backlog, we have just enough information to enable us to do what we need to do next and do it well. A useful backlog provides transparency to our entire organisation about what we are working on now, what is coming next, and what will happen in the future. It also provides the information on what is ready to be worked on immediately, and what requires more investigation or elaboration before it can be worked on.

A useful backlog is an immensely valuable tool, it enables us to make the best decisions possible, and take the right actions at the right time.

Keeping a backlog in a useful state is hard work. In Scrum, for instance, we have a Product Owner role whose primary responsibility is maintaining the backlog, and even in Scrum, this is often not enough. That's because maintaining, understanding, and benefiting from the backlog require a contribution from all the stakeholders involved.

An unruly backlog is expensive in a lot of ways.

So, the solution is simple, right? Throw away stuff that you don't need! If you are doing this, great for you, stop reading now.

But if you find your backlog is hard to maintain, it is a place where things go to die, and people are always resistant to throwing things away, the Not Now Backlog might just be the tool for you.

I will never quite understand people's aversion to throwing backlog items away. I believe if something is important, it will come back to the backlog later. And that if we haven't touched a User Story or a feature in the last two years, it's highly unlikely we will be working on it in the future. But I get surprisingly little support for this way of thinking. People worry about traceability, and that some piece of vital information may be lost. So, to soothe those fears, we have the Not Now Backlog.

First, you need to decide what 'now' means to your organisation. This can be a tricky question to answer, but I generally ask myself and my stakeholders a few questions:

- How far into the future can we reliably predict our priorities?
- How far into the future do we need to predict our priorities?
- How often do our priorities change drastically?
- How many items can we commit to maintaining?
- How much time and effort are we willing to spend on backlog maintenance?

This results in a lot of discussions, but in the end, what we need to arrive at is something like "we want to be able to see as far as X months/weeks/days into the future".

Once we reach that agreement, it is very simple: we go through our huge unruly backlog and ask ourselves "Do we realistically think this will be a priority within the next X months/weeks/days?". Everything that is a "No" goes into the Not Now Backlog.

Congratulations, you can now start focusing on bringing value to the backlog you have.

"But now we need to maintain that backlog too!" I hear you cry. The only thing I can say about that is, I never have. Every time I have used this tool, I have never again needed the items that were moved there, they simply went there to die. But luckily, we saved them just in case ;-).

In case I have not made it clear, this is a tool I think we should be able to do without; a suboptimal solution to what I consider a larger problem. But, maybe it's a necessary first step before we can get rid of those "just in case" items.

Tips

- If you are having trouble finding the now interval, just start with 6 months.
- Do not put things here that you know you're never going to do. If you can get everyone to agree it will never be done, throw it away.
- Try setting a work in progress limit instead of a time interval and simply say, the backlog never contains more than X items.
- Use this in environments where law or regulation mandates traceability.

Credit: This was originally created by a great friend and former co-worker of mine Christoffer Valgren: https:// retrospektivet.wordpress.com/. I think it was a response to my constant advocacy that we throw things away. Also, his original Swedish name for it is much better "glömskalista", which basically means "forget about list".

Visualised Flow

There is nothing more crucial to the success of a product than collaboration, at least that's what we believe in the Agile world. Collaboration is hard in any context, but it's basically impossible when people aren't even talking about the same things.

Are you having long, hot, and boring Sprint Planning meetings, it smells bad in the room, and in the end, everyone agrees to a Sprint Goal just to get out of there?

If the answer is yes, then Visualised Flow will likely help you a lot.

- Do your stakeholders know what you're working on at this moment?
- Do they know what you are going to work on next?
- Do they know if the things you have just finished are actually in production or not?
- Do they know what actions they need to take to get their items to the front of the queue?

If the answer to any these questions is no, then Visualised Flow will likely help you a lot.

This is one of the most steadfast and valuable tools in my toolkit. It is usually one of the first things I look for when I enter an organisation and one of my first objectives if it doesn't exist.

Not only can visualising the flow increase transparency of the work in progress, but it is built to facilitate and support decision making and collaboration across your organisation.

The goal is to visualise how value flows through your organisation, from the moment something is requested to the moment it arrives at the intended recipient. Anyone in your organisation should be able to glance at this tool and know what the status of an item is.

Find the In-Flows

First, I start out by trying to figure out where requests for work come from. Items don't just magically appear in the backlog, they originate from somewhere, whether this is specific stakeholders or different products will depend on your context. Some common examples are shown below.

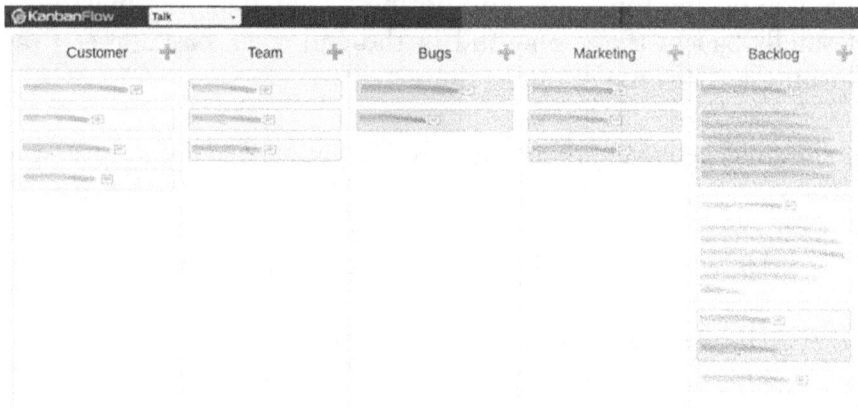

Figure 12 - Find the In-Flows

This allows our stakeholders to prioritise as individuals, to consider what is most important to them, but eventually, everything gets moved into the backlog area where we need to make decisions about how we will balance the conflicting priorities.

Visualising the prioritised in-flow of work helps facilitate the overall prioritisation discussions. Because it is impossible to ignore the priorities of the others, they are right there in front of us.

So we end up with a list of items that have been prioritised against one another, but these items are very rarely in a state where we can simply pull them and start working.

Refinement

Usually, some form of elaboration is required before items are ready to be worked on. Most people refer to this as refinement or grooming of the backlog. If you have a specific process in place for this, you can visualise it. If not, here is a very simple starting point.

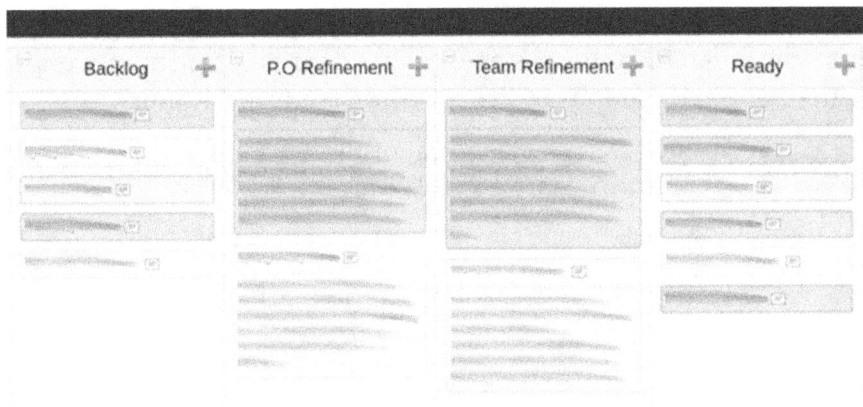

Figure 13 - Refinement process, from Backlog to Ready

In this example, we have items under investigation from the Product Owner and items that need investigation from the team; both can easily see things that are awaiting action from them.

Your process may be much more elaborate than this, maybe you require a customer sign off or UI mockups, or you have a prototyping phase. Regardless of what your process looks like, the objective here is to reach the "Ready" column, from where items can simply be pulled into implementation.

How the "Ready" column is defined will vary from organisation to organisation. I highly recommend you consider a formal "Definition of Ready" at this stage, but if you don't have that yet, a simple starting point is "all the team members agree we could work on this item tomorrow".

This is the state most people think of when they think of a backlog "Ready". The backlog "Ready" is simply the top of the backlog and features items that are ready to be worked on by the team.

Implementation

From the team's perspective, things are now much easier; we have a prioritised list that is defined by the level of detail that we require to actually work on it. We simply start pulling things into the implementation stage, maybe this is a Sprint if we are using Scrum, or simply In Process if we are using Kanban.

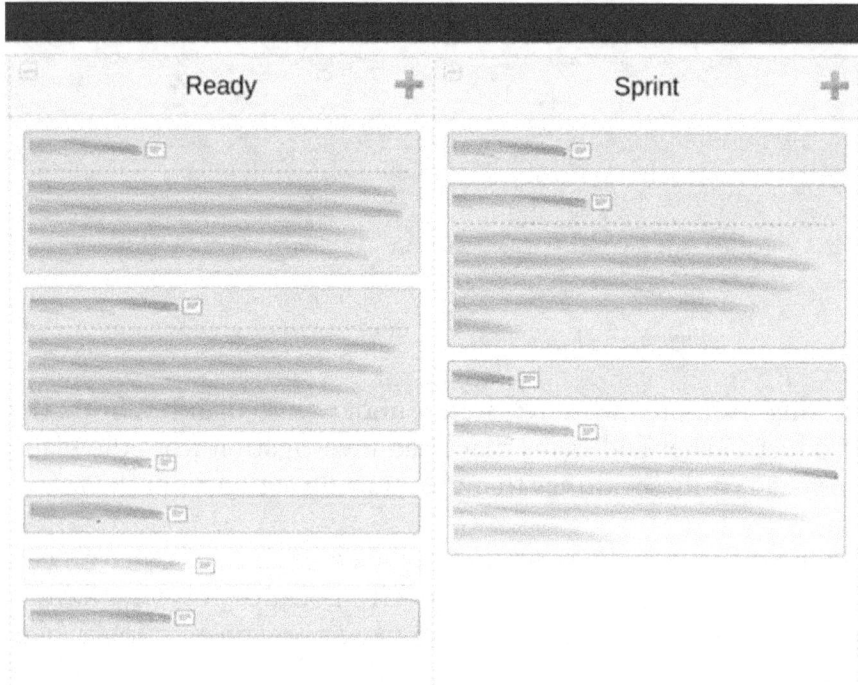

Figure 14 - Implementation: Items in progress

The Outflow

If you are practising continuous deployment or releasing to production at the end of each Sprint, then you can likely skip this step. Ideally, we all want to be in the situation that "Done" on the team's board means completely done, as in delivered to a customer who is happy with it, but not all teams are in that state yet.

If you are not yet at this stage, you need to also visualise what happens after items are done by the teams and before they are actually delivered.

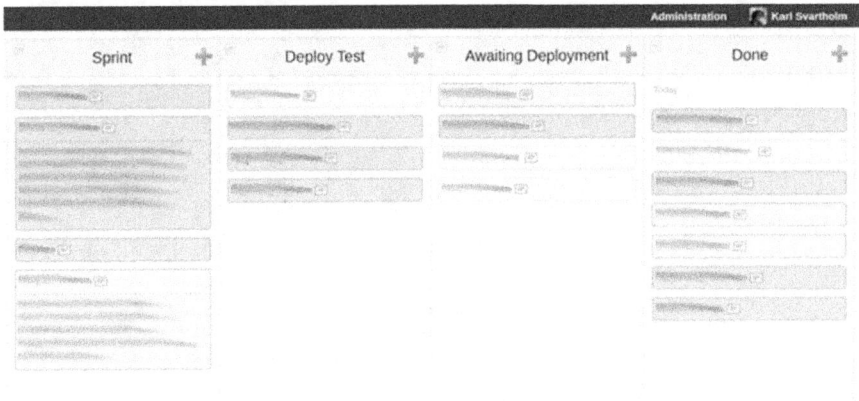

Figure 15 - *The Outflow, from implemented to production*

In this example, we have a "Deployment Test" phase, and then we hand over the Backlog items to the deployment team and because of that, we have a waiting area for Awaiting Deployment. In this example, the Awaiting Deployment step helps us because people start to ask questions like:

"Why are there so many items in the Awaiting Deployment column?"

"Well, if you recall we need to hand over our work to the deployment team because we don't have direct control over the servers. If we had that, we could move these waiting items much faster."

Regardless of what it looks like for you, you need to make each stage clear so that if items are not actually in production, everyone in your organisation can see that.

Seeing The Whole

Put it all together and what do you get? You get an overview of your organisation's entire process flow, the ability to make more informed decisions and have collaborations where everyone is talking about the same thing.

Figure 16 - Seeing the whole, our flow end-to-end
Seeing The Whole

Abstraction

A side benefit of this visualisation system is it allows abstraction where needed, which enables the management of backlog items at scale. Probably the development team has a team board that carries more specifics about each items breakdown and progress, but our entire organisation doesn't need this information. It would merely confuse them to have that level of detail, thereby reducing our transparency.

Never confuse visibility with transparency. Information can be highly visible, but if the person seeing it can't interpret it, it's not transparent.

The same of course goes for all stages here; maybe the Product Owner has a defined refinement process, maybe the deployment team does, all of that is visualised to appropriate detail here.

People and Interactions over Processes and Tools

It is very possible to setup this entire system and have no positive effect at all from it because this is a tool to facilitate conversations - not replace them. People understand how this visualisation works because they are involved in how it's created and used, they are present when their items are moved and elaborated. If you use this visual workflow as an excuse to not speak to each other, then the visualisation will not work, because the necessary conversations never happen.

Tips

- Use different colours to illustrate different inflows so they can easily be tracked throughout the process.
- If more detail is available for a specific stage, for example, a team's Scrum board, include where that information can be found in this flow.
- Value ease of use over functionality when choosing a tool to do this, I use http://www.kanbanflow.com
- If you don't know your process today, start simple and add the missing steps as you discover them.

Credit: The details in this tool are developed by myself; I have been iterating the design over many years and products. However, process visualisation has been around long enough I wouldn't even hazard a guess at who invented it.

Morning Meeting Protocol

Do your morning meetings meander? Are they unengaging and dull? Do people stand around waiting for the Scrum Master to point at them so they start talking? Does everyone recite off what they did yesterday like they're reading from a script?

If this seems familiar to you, then you might want to consider implementing a Morning Meeting Protocol.

A Morning Meeting Protocol is simply a collection of the items that are important to cover in your team's daily meeting. The goal of this protocol is to move away from simply having a morning meeting ceremony to solving real issues that your team faces. It also brings a structure and rhythm to the meeting that makes it feel a lot more productive. Finally, the structure is a great first step in building the muscle memory we want to make it. So eventually we don't need the protocol at all.

Here's an example to get you started:

Calendar	New actions

• What meetings did team members attend yesterday?
   ◦ Any actions for the team?
• What meetings do we have today?
   ◦ Do you need anyone for them?
• Do we have anything being delayed by meetings?
	• Production issues?
	• Any emails that came in?
	• Anything from Chat Rooms?
	• Any unplanned work?

What have we done?	What will we do?

• Sync board and Jira
   ◦ Is the "Definition of Done" met
• What have we done well?
• Is there anything blocked?
   ◦ What can we do to unblock it?
	• Who will do what?
	• Does anyone need help?
	• Have you communicated with who you should?
	• Do we have any experiments we should be doing?

Other	**Parking lot**
• Planned absences? • Monday = Health Check • Anything else you wanted to say?	• You can leave now if you like!

What your teams put in their Morning Meeting Protocol is entirely up to you and the team, but try to move away from simply having the standard reporting that usually makes the meetings unengaging and boring. Try to move the focus to what the team really needs to meet their goals, rather than treating this as another reporting tool. Use the example above as inspiration, but ask yourself the question "What is important for us to think about everyday?" As you go, update the protocol to include things that often get missed, but affect the team's performance.

Tips:

- Put the focus on the work to be done, not people reporting.
- Having the protocol displayed as a slideshow causes you to focus on only one topic at a time.
- While you review the pending topics, grab the items from the parking lot throughout the meeting.
- Help your team create this agenda themselves; they will be more invested in it!
- Change the protocol with items coming from the team

retrospectives.

Credit: This was invented by a great team I worked with at www.Meltwater.com

Work In Progress Protocol

I see many teams adopting Kanban, but not respecting the Work In Progress (WIP) limits they set. Kanban has very few rules, and choosing not to follow one - "Limit work in progress" - is bound to cause problems.

But people naturally wonder:

"Are we supposed to sit around and do nothing when we reach a made-up number on a whiteboard? That sounds a little crazy..."

That does sound a bit crazy, but that is not what Kanban is advocating at all. The way I see it, Kanban isn't trying to make us act blindly and without thought, quite the opposite, it's trying to make sure we stop and think before we simply start pulling more things into an already overcrowded work queue.

Kanban's mantra is:
"Stop starting and start finishing!"

So, what do we do instead of sitting on our hands? This is where the WIP Protocol comes into place. It's a simple set of things we try and consider before we even consider starting new work. Here's an example:

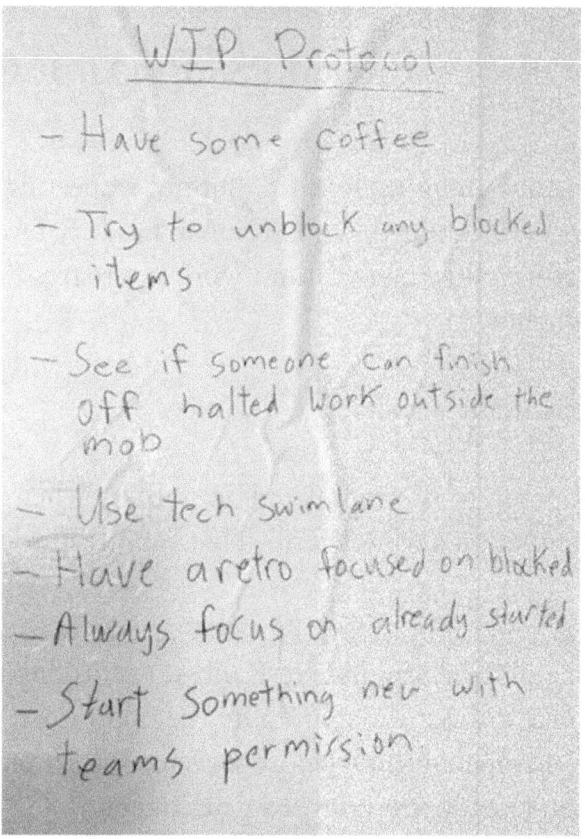

Figure 17 – Example of WIP protocol rules by one team

You can put anything you like on your list, just keep in mind that once you reach your WIP limit, starting to work on a new User Story or item is always the option of last resort. Finishing something you already started or preventing future occurrences of obstacles to work are much better options.

Powering through work is a sufficient strategy when something has a definitive end. If you're chopping a pile of wood for a few hours, it's generally not worth investing the time to optimise your workflow. You can just put your head down and power through it. But is your backlog coming to an end anytime soon? Are you running out of work to do? Of course not! In environments where work doesn't have a definitive end, powering through work will not help. The only way to get more done is to improve your ability to finish what you've already started. As long as you're busying yourself by starting more work, you are not investing in completing the work you've already started.

Tips:

- Place the WIP Protocol next to the team's Kanban board, so it is very visible.
- Review the WIP Protocol every so often to see if you can improve on it.
- Investigate how Kanban seeks to address issues of flow to improve on it further.
- Have your team create this protocol themselves; they will be more invested in it!
- Have "Start something new with team's permission" and "Discuss adjusting WIP limits" as the last options on the list.

Credit: As far as I am aware, this one was developed by me. If you know of a similar tool, ping me so that I add here the right credit to other authors.

Enjoyed? Why Not **Leave A Five Star Review On Amazon** And Help Us Help Other Scrum Masters?

At the time of first launch, the book was not yet available on Amazon. But by the time you are reading this text, chances are that the book is published on Amazon.

So, please help us spread the love by giving us 5 stars on Amazon.

Higher ratings help the book found by the people who will benefit from it the most.

Not 5 Stars?

If you think the book doesn't deserve 5 stars, let us know why via email to communications@oikosofy.com.

Please include subject line: AAT Review

We promise to read every email and do something about it. This will help us improve the next versions of the book.

If You Enjoyed Jeff's Actionable Agile Tools, You Will Love **Vasco's #NoEstimates!**

Download the free chapter of #NoEstimates, the book by Vasco Duarte.

Here's What You'll Learn In This Chapter
IT CAN BE THE DIFFERENCE BETWEEN A SUCCESSFUL LAUNCH AND A FAILED ONE...

- 2 Laws explaining what's wrong with making estimates (Why violating them could derail your whole project)
- The ONLY WAY to estimate and forecast a complex system like software development
- The MAIN reason why (contrary to popular beliefs) estimates are harmful for your project and your company?
- How a single code almost destroyed Apple's vaunted security and credibility (It COULD happen to your company, too)?
- 6 powerful laws explaining how unstable estimate really is
- Learn about "Death March Projects" and how it can ruin your team
- How to effectively predict when a project will end by asking only these 2 simple questions?

Download The FREE Chapter NOW!
You can also type this link in your browser:
bit.ly/NoEstimates-freechapter

www.ingramcontent.com/pod-product-compliance
Lightning Source LLC
Chambersburg PA
CBHW061158180526
45170CB00002B/848